LIVE A LIFE OF ENCOURAGEMENT

A LIFE *to* LIVE

30 POEMS *for* 30 DAYS

STEVE NAPIER

ISBN 979-8-218-42832-7 (paperback)

ACKNOWLEDGEMENTS

This book would not have been possible without the following influences in my life: GOD, my heavenly father. From him my talent was given. Paula Napier, my amazing wife. She stands beside me and is always encouraging. Jonathan "Coach JC" Conneely, friend and mentor. He had me write down my top 10 dreams and has not let me give up on them.

MY WHY BEHIND MY WHAT

The reason I took time to put these words to paper was to encourage myself never to give up. I am surrounded by people that are constantly encouraging me to chase my dreams. I shared some of my writings with them and they persuaded me to share them with the world. I encourage everyone to find people that will do what the people in my life are doing for me. I hope you enjoy the words that GOD placed on my heart.

CHASE YOUR DREAMS

There are people from afar

That will say you are crazy

For chasing after your dreams,

But they are just jealous and lazy.

Reach for what you want,

Take pride in what you do.

Turn away from the old ways

And aspire for something new.

The path is straight ahead

Directed to your destiny;

Living a full life,

Is not fantasy but reality.

KEEP WORKING HARD

Does your heart beat faster

As a deadline draws near?

Do you feel like you're behind?

Are you overcome by fear

That you won't get done,

The things that you have planned?

Put your nose to the grindstone,

And work as hard as you can.

You have to put in the work.

So, there is no need to perspire;

You will finish on time,

With the things you desire.

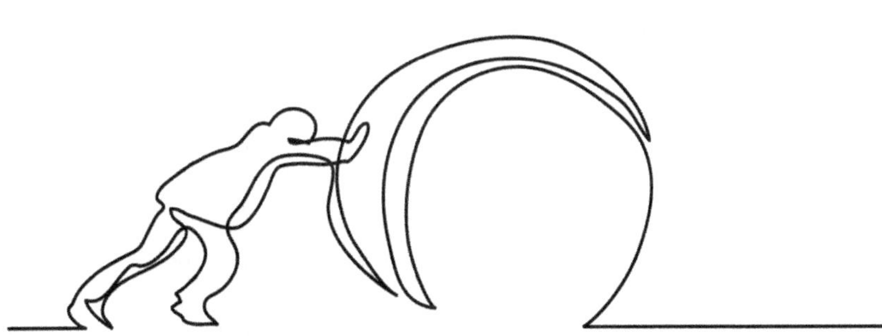

REACHING MY DREAMS

I am reaching one of my dreams.

In case you don't know it,

I am bound and determined

To become a published poet.

I am closer to my goal!

The mountaintop is in my sight;

I am dedicated to the vision.

I have to finish the fight.

The goal was written down;

New work is beginning.

The next series will be

On relationships winning.

PLAN YOUR DAY WELL

Brighten up your morning,

By planning out your day.

Be consistent in your actions

So you can start to say

I have a vision set for my life.

I will finish what I begin,

I will repeat the proven process,

So I can constantly win.

STEP BY STEP TO GET THERE

Taking the daily steps,

Doing the daily grind,

Puts you closer to the goal.

There's no reason to look behind

At the things you no longer chase,

And a lifestyle you no longer crave.

You had to give them up.

Now they're buried in a grave,

Keep the focus on your vision,

And the dreams that you cast,

To become the results of your future,

And no longer a victim of your past.

PERSEVERE TO THE END

The world is your boxing ring

And your life is a championship bout.

Are you going the full distance?

Or are you going out for the count?

Don't ever throw in the towel

Because you got knocked down.

A winner is a prizefighter

That can go another round.

Preserve through the training;

It all worth it in the end.

When your bout is finally over,

You will have the victory to win.

A MAN ON A MISSION

Motivated to be great,

And pushed by my best,

There's no room for second thoughts.

There is no time for rest;

I've got to get up and move,

And make the most of day.

Victory is mine to have.

So get out of my way;

I'm a man on a mission

With no end in sight.

On my way to the top

Through the struggles,

I will face all,

To get up to the mountain,

To swim across the sea,

To reach all of my goals,

And to be the best version of me.

“We rise
by lifting
others.”

WHAT YOU NEED TO SUCCEED

When trying something new

Others will look to find what's wrong.

Remove them from your circle;

People like that don't belong.

Not looking for some "Yes Men"

Feedback is what you need

To grow from where you are

Down to a path to succeed.

IT'S NEVER AN ATTACK

As we conquer a challenge,

Another may come our way.

Were the previews for training?

For whatever we're facing today,

Don't look at it as an attack;

It can be a chance to grow.

Embarking on something new,

Learning what we did not know,

And some extraordinary thinking

Can conquer ordinary strife.

We all are given a chance

Not to live a so-called normal life.

FAILURE IS A CHANCE

If trial and error

Can lead you to succeed,

Why do so many give up

Before they ever reach their dreams?

Failure is not the end;

It's a chance for you to create

A different way of doing things,

A time for you to innovate.

You can always perfect a skill,

You can always become elite,

It doesn't happen overnight;

Some processes you have to repeat.

Keep a winning mindset,

Hone your skills and ability,

Go out and achieve your goals

And then your vision becomes your reality.

"Instead of giving
yourself a reason why you
can't, give yourself a reason
of why you can."

QUESTIONS YOU NEED TO ANSWER

When the last page is written

And your life is no more

What will your legacy be?

What will you be remembered for?

Where were your priorities at?

Was your marriage and family number one?

Were you investing in their future?

Were they the reason everything was done?

Were the sacrifices that you made,

Purposeful and planned?

Did you lead them from the front?

Always do what you can;

So I will ask this again:

When your life is no more

What will your legacy be?

What will you be remembered for

"Don't be ashamed of a scar.
It simply means that you
are stronger than whatever
tried to hurt you."

GET UP AND DO YOUR WORK

Arise and shine, everyone;

A new day has begun!

Get your day started;

Let's go for a little run.

Get your heart quickly beating,

As sweat forms on your brow.

There's no time like the present;

Don't put off what can be done now.

A mile cannot be reached

Without a first step being taken.

If a marathon is your goal,

You have to complete the training.

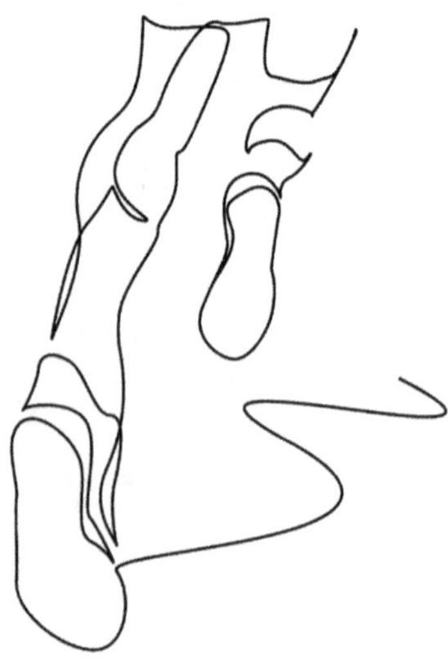

NO STOPPING

Iron sharpens iron,

Brothers locked arm in arm,

We are battle-tested warriors

Positioned on the front lines.

We are men of valor;

Courage is in our blood.

The weak will be protected

For we are always standing up.

Against us, the war has been waged.

But standing united, we won't be defeated;

The victory lies ahead of us.

We are not stopping until we succeed.

SOAR HIGHER

Race to the highest mountain,

We reach for the tallest peak,

We do it for ourselves first.

Self-accomplishment is what we seek;

We don't do it for the glory

Even though that can be great

With our circle cheering us on,

So that we don't try to procrastinate,

In turning our dreams into reality

And making them obtained one by one.

Then on to the next dream,

Until each of them is done.

Then we will make a brand new list,

Reaching higher than ever before,

Because we will be like eagles,

And above the clouds, we will soar.

"Courage isn't having the strength to go on. It is going on when you don't have strength."

– Napoleon Bonaparte

LIVE TO YOUR FULLNESS

Stop the could of, should of, and would of,

Stop the if only what might have been,

And start living to your full potential.

Start planning on stacking your wins,

And be under your purpose.

Stay driven to your vision

While living out your calling,

And being a man on his mission.

PLANNING AHEAD OF TIME

Not wanting to rush the time,

I'm not worried about counting the days.

My future is the road ahead

And filled with very amazing things.

My vision had to be cast;

Goals were needed to be achieved.

I wrote down my top ten dreams,

To accomplish what I believed.

So the progress you have seen

Come from what I did in the dark.

So, are you coming along for the ride

Or are you spinning your wheels in the park?

SELF-EVALUATION

It's the end of work week.

How did I spend my time?

Did I complete all my tasks?

What hidden talents did I find?

Did I work on my book?

Did I write a brand-new song?

Did I complete my dreams?

How's the process coming along?

Was there time spent with family?

Did I spend time loving my wife?

Did I invest in my purpose?

Did I invest in my life?

MOTIVATION

A brotherhood was formed,

A circle was created,

We will stack wins daily

Because we all need to be motivated.

We look to see others win,

We push others to succeed,

We all have our vision,

We all created our creed.

As we climb up the mountain,

As we scale the tallest peak,

We will cheer each other on

Cause Victory is what we seek.

WHEN IS THE FINAL TIME?

The hunger and thirst,

Do they ever stop?

Are you always climbing?

Do you ever reach the top?

Once you reach your goal,

Does it mean you've finished the race?

Is it time for slowing down

Or do you need to pick up your pace?

For tomorrow is never promised;

Today is always a gift.

Do you need to be present in the now?

In case others may need a lift,

It is never considered a handout,

It is meant to lift others.

Do we pour out of our abundance

So we can fill another's cup?

"Everything you need
to accomplish your goals
is already inside you."

DREAM AND WORK

Dare to dream and follow the mission,

Live a life that is fueled by a vision,

Pursue your goals to achieve the prize,

Never give up to the top you'll rise.

Putting in the work is what others won't see;

They won't see the sacrifices you made

for what you believe.

Some may get jealous and that is okay,

Don't get distracted by what they might say.

At the end of the road you will have no regrets.

All, whispering to you, is always a winning bet.

"It always seems impossible
until it's done."

– Nelson Mandela

ROADS TO GOALS

Roads that lead to the goals
are not meant for the weak,
Daily putting into action
the words that you speak,
Build a strong foundation
that withstands the test of time.
Pursuing your calling
will be a constant grind.
Focus on your future
and the things that you want to achieve,
For visions to become reality,
you must first have to believe
That you will always keep a heart
that is full of desire.
The passion that is inside of you
is the fuel for the fire.

"Our greatest glory is not in never failing, but in rising every time we fail."

– Confucius

TIME COUNTS

Are you alive or just breathing air?

Going through the motions totally unaware,

Time is fading away in the blink of an eye;

One moment you are born,

the next you're saying goodbye.

Your dreams and desires are what lie up ahead,

Make them your reality by doing what you said.

Lies of your past don't define who you are,

Shoot for the moon while reaching for the stars.

NO DISTRACTIONS

What life do you want?

What is your game plan

To achieve your goals

And to become that man?

The obstacles will come;

They'll be right in your face.

But don't let them distract you

From winning your race.

PUT IN YOUR BEST TODAY

Up in the morning to start your day,

With positive thoughts as you go on your way,

Nothing in life will hold you back

To become the best with the wins you stack.

Moving the needle as you follow the plan,

Giving up things that you no longer desire,

Vision is the fuel that will ignite the fire

Inside your heart as you run the race.

To finish strong you must pick up the pace.

Not promised tomorrow but you are alive today.

Give it your best and you can proudly say,

Victory is mine and I have reached my goal

Because putting in work will never get old.

"Hardships often prepare ordinary people for an extraordinary destiny."

– C.S. Lewis

PUT IT IN ACTION

What is your goal?

What is your plan?

Are you putting in the work

Or are you falling behind?

It's time to get busy,

Have some skin in the game,

Excuses will do nothing.

Things will always stay the same

If the plan is to succeed

And the vision has been made.

Let's put it all into action

So the dream doesn't fade.

DON'T LIVE A WASTED LIFE

Are you moving forward?

Are you gaining ground?

Are you reaching your goals?

Are you glory-bound?

Start saving for tomorrow,

Start investing in today,

Tighten up your circle

As you go along the way.

Live life to the fullest,

Don't live one of the regrets,

And don't let past failures become a prison;

A bright future is what's next.

THE WINNING PLANS

It's a beginning of a new week,

Plans to win have been set.

Having scheduled out my days,

I will live with no regrets.

Chance will not be missed,

Opportunities will be gained,

When the sun doesn't shine,

I will dance in the rain.

I will not be distracted

By the words that are said;

I will relish in the victories.

Every night I go to bed,

I will focus on my goals,

With statement and dates,

With my timelines being set,

Will make it impossible to procrastinate.

I will elevate my dreams

To the highest levels

So they are always reached

Because I refuse to settle.

"Your life is a
message to the world.
Make it inspiring."

GET PREPARED FIRST

Before you climb

You must prepare

To take the journey

To thinner air.

Acclimate your body

And strengthen your mind

Because you can do it.

It's just a matter of time.

Set a lofty goal,

You will reach the top.

Even though setbacks will come,

There's no reason to stop.

So plant your flag

When you have reached the peak.

"I did it and I made it,"

These are the words you will speak.

"Build the strongest you!"

Episode 63 – Win All Day Podcast
Coach JC

WHAT YOU NEED TO KNOW

First, know your why.

Know why you exist,

And have a Mission that is planned.

Then stay focused on the things you have planned,

And daily do what you can.

Then figure out the what;

The purpose behind the Vision,

 Keeping focused on the goals,

And confident in your decisions.

Principles are what you stand for

And who you need to become.

Stop letting the world change them,

And taking you out of the race you run.

So with Mission, Vision, and Principles,

You can become the greatest M.V.P,

Living a life full of purpose,

And encouraging others in themselves to believe.

"Life us 10% of what happens to you and 90% how you react to it."

Charles R. Swindoll

WHAT MAKES UP YOUR LIFE?

Is your life filled with hope?

Are you pursuing your dreams?

Is your life lived by faith,

For things yet to be seen?

Live life with a clear vision:

One driven by your purpose.

Even though this world may be falling into chaos,

There's no reason to focus on that circus.

ABOUT THE AUTHOR

Steve Napier was born and raised in Tulsa, Oklahoma. He currently resides in Coweta, Oklahoma with his lovely wife. They spend their leisure time enjoying the beauty of nature. Since 2012, he has been serving in a ministry that is impacting the lives of men in his local community. One of his current pursuits has him involved in a personal development mastermind group.